Sea Otter Goes Hunting

Story by Beverley Randell
Illustrations by Julian Bruère

One day, a little sea otter
knew that he was old enough
to find food for himself.

He wasn't a baby any more.
He didn't have to ride
on his mother's chest
or swim beside her all the time.

He had learned how to dive
all the way down
to the bottom of the sea.
That was where he could hunt
for shellfish.

The little sea otter rolled over and dived down.

Tiny bubbles of air in his thick fur made him look shiny as he flashed through the water.

As soon as he reached the mud and the rocks at the bottom, he saw something bright. He picked it up with his front paws and rushed up to the top again.

But he had made a mistake.
He had not picked up a shellfish.
He had found an empty drink can!

It was bright and shiny,
and was fun to play with.
But it wasn't good to eat.

The little sea otter dropped the can
and dived down again.

He put his paws between the rocks
and felt around.
He found a shellfish! It was a clam.
But he could not move it.
The clam was tightly stuck.

The little sea otter
had to come up for air.

Then he dived down to try again.
He saw another clam.
And this time, when he tugged at it,
it came away in his paws.
He tucked it under his arm
and rushed up to the top again.

The little sea otter
lay on his back in the waves
and tried to open the clam
with his teeth.
But the shell stayed tightly closed.

Then he remembered
how his mother opened clam shells.
She always used a rock!

So the little sea otter dived down
to the bottom of the sea again.

He had to keep holding
onto the clam.
He didn't want to lose it.

He hunted around in the seaweed
and saw a rock that he could use.
When he came back up again,
he was carrying
the rock and the clam.

By now he was feeling tired.
Hunting for food was hard work!

Then he lay on his back
and put the rock down on his front.
He knew just what to do
because he had often watched
his mother.

He held the clam in both paws
and hammered it against the rock.

The clam still didn't open,
so he had to keep trying.
He hammered again,
and again, and again.

Crack!
The shell broke open at last.
Now the hungry little sea otter
was able to eat the clam.
It was delicious!
And he had found it and opened it,
all by himself.